STUNT WORK
AND
STUNT PEOPLE

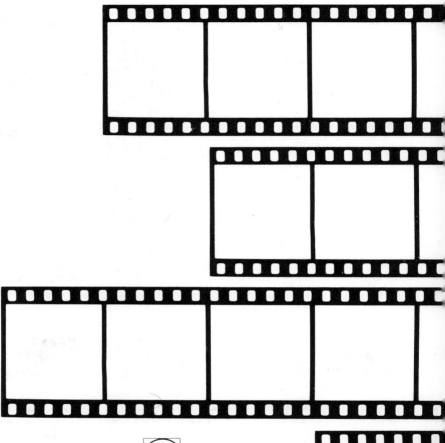

Franklin Watts
New York/London/Sydney/Toronto/1982
A Triumph Book

STUNT WORK

AND

STUNT PEOPLE

CAROL A. EMMENS

Photographs courtesy of: Harry Madsen: pp. 6 and
51; United Press International, Inc.: pp. 11, 14, 15;
Vic Magnotta: p. 22–23; Victoria Vanderkloot: p.
32; Museum of Modern Art/Film Stills Archive/
Copyright © by Universal City Studios, Inc. Courtesy of MCA Publishing, a Division of MCA Inc.:
pp. 46 and 60; John Epper: p. 69; American Humane Association: p. 73; Jeannie Epper/Joan
Alden: p. 80.

R.L. 2.9. Spache Revised Formula

Library of Congress Cataloging in Publication Data

Emmens, Carol A.
Stunt work and stunt people.

(A Triumph book)
Includes index.
Summary: Reveals many techniques used
to perform movie and television stunts and
discusses aspects of a stunt double's career.
1. Stunt men and women—Juvenile literature.
[1. Stunt men and women] I. Title.
PN1995.9.S7E4   791.43′028   81-21824
ISBN 0-531-04411-4   AACR2

CONTENTS

7039315

For my son Scott

This book is based almost entirely on interviews with stunt men and women. Without their generous help I would not have been able to write it. My thanks to Colette Alexander, Sandy Alexander, David Ellis, Andy Epper, Gary Epper, Jeannie Epper, John Epper, Stephanie Epper, Tony Epper, Duffy Hambleton, Gene Hartline, Hank Hooker, Gray Johnson, Hubie Kerns, Hubie Kerns, Jr., Vic Magnotta, Bob Minor, Kitty O'Neil and her husband—Tom Justice, Dar Robinson, Spanky Spangler, Paul Stader, Alex Stevens, Jerry Summers, Victoria Vanderkloot, Hank Wills, and Bob Yerkes.

My thanks to pilots Jim Appleby, Frank Pine, Ross Reynolds, and Art Scholl.

My thanks to Al Griswold, a special effects expert, and Nick Fiorentino, a film buff.

My special thanks to stunt man Harry Madsen.

GO FOR IT!

Last year he was beaten, knifed, and shot. He cracked up his car and he turned over his van. He fell 40 feet (12.2 m) to the ground. He was set on fire. And he liked every minute of it! He is Harry Madsen. He is one of the top 200 stunt men and women who work in movies and TV shows. Suppose a script calls for a character to do something dangerous, like falling out a window. Then the stunt people fill in for, or "double," the actors. The stunt doubles are trained to do the dangerous movie and TV work without getting hurt.

The stunt doubles have to be about the same weight and height as the performers. They sometimes wear "fat suits" to double performers who are heavy. The stunt doubles are usually seen from a distance so they do not have to look like the performers. Sometimes men even double for women! The stunt doubles wear wigs and the same costumes as the performers. On the screen they look like the performers. And sometimes the performers say they did their own stunts!

The stunt doubles plan and practice all their stunts, which they call "gags." They are not daredevils. They do not risk their lives to do one wild stunt. David Ellis said that stunt doubles "have to be able to do the gag over and over. We have to be able to make the stunt look good and make it safe."

Of course, there is always a chance a stunt will go wrong. There is always a chance a stunt double will get hurt. But stunt doubles learn to live with danger. They do all kinds of stunts under all kinds of conditions. Or as they say, they "go for it."

STEP ON IT!

"Step on it," yells Boss Hogg as he and his deputy Roscoe drive after the Duke boys on the TV show "The Dukes of Hazzard." The show always ends with a wild car chase. They crash into trees, fire hydrants, or shopping baskets. They jump over fences, smash through roadblocks, and land in ponds. But the stars are not the drivers of the cars. Stunt men drive for them. Jerry Summers is the number one stunt driver for the show. He also plans the car stunts.

As many as ten cars are used to film one chase for "The Dukes of Hazzard." They are not like ordinary cars. They are "rigged," or rebuilt, to protect the drivers. The roofs of the cars are lined with steel bars, called roll bars. They come up along the roof and down the seat. They keep the roofs from caving in when the cars roll over or flip over. For "heavy," or dangerous, stunts, the insides of the cars are lined with full steel "cages." They are like roll bars, but they also go around the steering wheel, the two front seats, and the front window.

The drivers make the cars as safe as they can. They use new shocks and tires. They also use special seat belts to hold themselves in the car when it stops short or crashes. Things that stick out, like handles, are removed. Often the gas tank is removed and replaced with a small nonbreakable tank. Sometimes the cars are padded, and usually the drivers wear pads and sometimes a helmet.

Car stunts must be planned carefully because the drivers go at high speeds to make the chases look real. Gary Epper has driven for police shows like "Starsky and Hutch" and private-eye shows like "Charlie's Angels" and "Vega$." He said every step of every car chase is planned the same way every step of every stage dance is planned.

But the stunts are still dangerous, and mistakes do happen. For a TV pilot, or trial show, Dick Butler drove a 1947 jeep across a field. Buddy Joe Hooker and Stephanie Epper were in the back seat. When Dick reached the place where he planned to stop, the director yelled, "Keep going!" Dick did. Then suddenly the jeep hit a ditch hidden by tall grass. Stephanie said, "We were going 45 mph [72.4 kmph] when suddenly the jeep came to a stop. Out I went, 15 feet [4.6 m] into the air." She hit her head and was in the hospital for ten days. She needed 75 stitches for the cuts on her leg. Dick was cut slightly, and Buddy Joe was able to jump out of the jeep without getting hurt.

Chases through real city streets need very carefully planning. Often the police help the stunt drivers. It took Alex Stevens weeks to plan the exciting car chase in the movie *The French Connection*. It was done on the streets of New York. The stunt drivers made large cardboard street maps and used toy cars to run through the chase. Then they practiced in their real cars, but they drove slowly. When they were ready, they filmed the chase in small parts called "takes."

Three look-alike, or duplicate, cars were used for the chase.

In almost all movie and TV chases the cars crash into things. On "The Dukes of Hazzard" Boss Hogg and Roscoe sometimes hit a fire hydrant. But it is not real. It is a prop made out of plastic. The Duke boys usually drive through a fence. It, too, is not real. It is made out of a lightweight wood that breaks easily. In most cases the objects stunt drivers hit are fake props.

Once in a while, though, the props are real. In the science fiction movie thriller *Scanners*, Alex Stevens drove a bus up a ramp. It flew through the air and crashed into the front window of a record store. The bus turned over and it slid on its roof for 90 feet (27.4 m). It broke over 8,000 real records!

Car chases on city streets
can be difficult. For this stunt,
Harry Madsen drove up a hidden
ramp to overturn his car.

Cars often crash through fake glass windows. In the movie *Four Friends* the crash through the window was more exciting than usual. Victoria Vanderkloot drove a 1953 Studebaker convertible through a second-story window. She drove through the window and down a very steep ramp. Cardboard boxes and rubber mats were stacked up on both sides of the ramp. They kept the car from flipping over on its back.

On the screen, cars often crash into other cars. On police shows like "Chips" as many as ten cars are dented or completely wiped out each week. But sometimes the same car is used several times. First the right fender is dented, then the left.

When cars crash in the movies, they are usually hit at one end or the other. Often the ground is wet and the car spins. Once in a while the center of the car is hit. This is called "T-boning." To protect the drivers, their sides of the cars are never hit. The strong force of the crash would hurt them, especially their backs.

One of the most dangerous stunts is crashing a car into a tractor-trailer truck. The impact is strong and the car goes right under the trailer. In the police movie *The Seven-ups* Jerry Summers drove a car into the back of a truck. He drove at 50 mph (80.5 kmph). The front of the car was padded, and he crashed into a padded wall hidden under the truck. The top of the car had been cut ahead of time, and it came off as the car hit the trailer. If Jerry had not ducked in time, he would have lost his head.

On the screen a car chase often ends because the "bad guy's" car goes over a cliff and bursts into flames. The stunt doubles, of course, are not in the car. They drive to the edge of the cliff and stop. There they are replaced by dummies. The special effects experts put gasoline "bombs" in the car. Often the car is sent over the cliff on a track or runner to control where it goes. When the car reaches the bottom of the cliff, the bombs are set off by remote control.

Small, rear-end fires are sometimes set off while the stunt doubles are still driving. A sheet of safety glass is put behind their seats. It protects them from the flames. As extra protection, the doubles also wear fire-resistant clothes.

The car chase through the streets of San Francisco in the police movie *Bullitt* is famous. It ended with a real bang as the killer's car crashed into a gas pump. The car, the pump, and then the whole gas station went up in flames. Stunt man Carey Loftin was behind the wheel.

But he was not behind the wheel of the car that crashed. He was behind the wheel of his own car. He used a steel bar to link the side of his car to the side of the crash car. He towed the crash car in the direction of the pump. When the crash car was close to it, he set it free. It ran into the gas pump, and the gasoline bombs were set off by remote control.

To add to the excitement of a chase, cars sometimes roll over and over. A piece of equipment called a cannon ram is used to make a car

Duffy Hambleton rolls over this 1967 Oldsmobile for the made-for-TV movie The Story of Kitty O'Neil. *The car was destroyed, but Duffy was not hurt.*

roll several times. A tube that looks like a cannon is put under the car or on the side of the car at an angle. Inside the cannon, or tube, is explosive powder. A pole that looks like a telephone pole is placed in the cannon. When the driver sets off the powder by a switch on the dashboard, the force of the explosion pushes the pole out. The force of the pole as it hits the ground pushes the car up and over.

Hal Needham made the first cannon ram, which is also called Needham's ram. Once a stunt man, he is now a director. He directed several movies that starred Burt Reynolds, including *Smokey and the Bandit*. Needham first tested his cannon ram during a car chase in the movie *McQ*. The powder in the cannon blew the car 20 feet (6.1 m) into the air. When the car landed, it rolled over eight times. Needham ended up with a broken back. The rams were later made less dangerous. Yet many stunt drivers still hurt their backs because the force of the explosion is great.

Duffy Hambleton holds the world record for rolling a car over. For the TV special "Super Stunts II" his car rolled over 17 times. He used enough powder in the cannon ram to fill five sticks of dynamite. Even he did not know the exact number of times the car would roll over.

To make a car roll over only once or twice a ramp is used. The driver drives the car up a ramp. At the end of the ramp the driver turns the wheel of the car to the far right or left. The sharp turn makes the car roll off the ramp. The ramps are most often 30–36 inches (76.2–91.4 cm) high and 12 feet (3.7 m) long, or about twice the length of the car's wheel-base. There are all kinds of ramps for all kinds of stunts.

Ramps are used to make one car ride over the top of another car or to make a car jump. The ramps are hidden or disguised. The car is driven up a ramp, sails through the air, and lands on the ground. Sometimes the car lands on a second ramp, or landing ramp.

Gray Johnson made a long 120-foot (36.6-m) jump down a hill on the TV show "Enos." At one point he was 25 feet (7.6 m) off the ground. Sand was placed in the back of the car. The sand balanced the weight of the engine in the front of the car. Without the sand the car would have

Left: Hal Needham is behind the wheel of this car as it travels up a ramp on a wharf. The car jumped 63 feet (19 m) and landed on a barge in the Arkansas River. Sand on the barge stopped it from going further. Needham was the stunt double for Burt Reynolds in the movie White Lightning.

Above: After Hal Needham completed his stunt, Burt Reynolds returned to his role as a convict in White Lightning.

landed nose first because the engine makes the front of the car heavier than the back. The car also had air seats and special shock absorbers to protect Gray.

Rocket cars are built to look like a rocket on its side. They are the fastest cars in the world. They are able to go over 600 mph (970 kmph). In the movie *Hooper* a rocket car went up a ramp and sailed over 400 feet (122 m). It slammed nose down into the ground and rolled over, end over end. Yet no one was hurt. Behind the wheel of the car sat a dummy! The car was worked by remote control. But Buddy Joe Hooker made two test runs in the car. He was the first stunt man to jump a rocket car. The first time he jumped the car he went 197 feet (60 m). The second time he jumped it he went 203 feet (61.9 m).

Sometimes drivers jump their cars into water. Those are the most dangerous car stunts. In the movie comedy *What's Up, Doc?* four Volkswagens were driven off a pier at the end of a wild and funny car chase. Then the fun ended for one of the drivers, Paul Stader. The front window of his car broke when it hit the water, which poured into it.

The car sank 40 feet (12.2 m) and Paul sank with it. He had a hard time getting out of the car. He was below the water for 2 minutes and 30 seconds. Most people last only 30 to 45 seconds without air. Luckily, Paul had trained himself to hold his breath longer for water stunts. But he still almost lost his life. He just made it to the top in time!

Now stunt doubles wear small air tanks around their necks when they crash into water. They also carry two large air tanks in the car. Divers stand by to help them as well. Yet, even with air tanks and safety divers on hand, many drivers have had close calls under the water.

On "Games People Play," a TV show, Spanky Spangler made a record 232-foot (70.7-m) jump. He landed in 15 feet (4.6 m) of water in Firebird Lake in Arizona. He had an air tank with him, but he had a hard time getting it on. He also landed in mud, and he had to cut his way out of it. His divers were getting ready to go after him just as he finally got to the top of the water.

Dar Robinson drove a bus off a long ramp for the movie *Night Hawks*. He jumped the bus 104 feet (31.7 m) and landed in the East River in

New York City at midnight. He drove the bus from behind a barrier to protect himself from the front window, which broke. The water was very cold; it was 38° F (3° C). The East River flows very fast, and Dar was 70 feet (21.3 m) below the top. Because of the danger of the fast-moving river, Dar waited for the divers to reach him. He had to wait several frightening minutes before the divers found him. Then they went to the top together.

Many things can go wrong when a car crashes into water. The front window can break from the crash. The car can land in mud. The drivers can lose their sense of direction when the car rolls over. And, worst of all, drivers never know which problem they will run into! It is not surprising that car crashes into water are among the most dangerous stunts.

ALL IN A
DAY'S WORK

She swung her fist at him. He slapped her face. Then he grabbed her and threw her to the ground. She moaned. She tried to push herself up. He kicked her. "Cut!" The scene was finished. For Sandy Alexander and Colette Alexander it was all in a day's work for the movie *Fame*.

Fighting, running, and falling are gags that are done often for all kinds of movies and TV shows. Although stunt doubles call them "light gags," they are not as easy as they look. The stunts take strength and practice.

For a fight the stunt doubles plan all the moves and practice over and over. They must make the fight look real, but they never really hit each other. Hubie Kerns said the way the camera is set up is important. He was the double for Adam West, who played Batman on TV. He often fought Batman's enemy Penguin and other "bad guys" so he knows all the secrets of TV fights. He said, "I face you. The camera is behind you or behind me. I throw a punch across your face, not towards you, but just across it. My fist goes in front of your face and past the camera. When you snap your head back, I throw my fist straight past your head to your ear. If the camera is at the side of us, it is seen as a miss. From behind us, it looks like a hit. But it takes a lot of practice to do it.

John Forster made a mistake in a fight and ended up with a very sore mouth. "The only time I got hurt was in a fight scene in *Buffalo Bill and the Indians*," he said. I leaned into a punch when I should have pulled back. I ended up with a broken jaw."

Professional fighters are usually not good TV and movie fighters. They keep their arms close to their bodies and throw fast punches. The camera cannot "see" the punches. Stunt doubles throw long, slow punches.

Sometimes several stunt doubles fight at once in scenes like street riots or barroom brawls. They need to practice carefully so they do not get in each other's way or hit the wrong double. The stunt doubles practiced the riot scene in the movie *Fort Apache, The Bronx* for three hours.

On shows like "The Incredible Hulk" or "Wonder Woman" the "bad guys" often hit the "good guys" over the head with hard objects such as chairs, rocks, or bottles. If stunt doubles were hit with real objects, they would be hurt. Instead they are hit with copies of bottles, chairs, and rocks, which are called props. These props are made to break easily in fight scenes.

Heavy paper, plastic, and styrofoam are used to make fake lamps, dishes, rocks, chairs, and other objects. Balsa wood is also used often to

Over: Craig Baxley throws Vic Magnotta through a balsa wood door in The Warriors.

make chairs, tables, boards, walls, and even houses. It is a light wood that is used for model airplanes, too. The wood is usually cut lightly to make it break. Real nails are never used. The chairs and tables are glued together. Even so, stunt doubles sometimes get hurt if they do not hit the fake walls or tables in the right spot.

Most fake glass is made from plastic that snaps into pieces. When movies began in the 1920s, fake glass was made from sugar and hot water. When water was poured on it, the fake glass melted. It also melted under the bright lights needed for the cameras. But it *was* good for eating! It was called candy glass. Today, fake glass is still known as candy glass, but the plastic glass is much better than the sugar-and-water glass. It does not melt.

Its name makes candy glass sound harmless. But it is not. Duffy Hambleton said, "It can put a lump on your head or even split it open." He knows. He was Robert Blake's double on the police show "Baretta," and he was often hit on the head.

Candy glass cuts, too. It does not cut like real glass. The cuts are dull and they are not deep. The danger of candy glass is the way it breaks. Jeannie Epper said, "It breaks into tiny pieces that you can get in your eyes." When stunt doubles crash through windows, they put their hands up in front of their faces or they bend their heads down.

Candy glass presents another problem. It sometimes causes the stunt doubles to slide. On "Wonder Woman" Jeannie Epper doubled the star, Lynda Carter. Jeannie once jumped through a window made out of candy glass. Then she slid on a piece of it and almost hit her head on the floor.

Candy glass is not always used for stunts. For very large windows, candy glass cannot be used because it is too heavy. David Ellis crashed through a real stained glass church window on a hang glider in the movie *Fooling Around*. The window was 45 feet (13.7 m) wide across the center, or diameter. David was well protected from the real glass. He wore a thick rubber mask of Gary Busey's face, the star he doubled. He also wore a helmet, small goggles over his eyes, and a wet suit under his clothes. Wet suits are thick rubber suits made for diving. They are very good for stunt work because they soften falls.

Like fights, low falls are all in a day's work for stunt doubles. The best way to fall is to touch down lightly on your hand, turn your head, and roll onto your shoulder. It sounds easy, but it is often made hard. Stunt doubles not only fall to the ground, they also fall over chairs, off cars, or down stairs. One stunt man said that all the falls he has taken have left his shoulders and knees in poor shape.

Some stunt doubles have broken their legs or ankles falling down stairs. But Hubie Kerns said that stair falls are "very, very easy" for anyone who learns the secrets of them and practices. Hubie said, "One trick is to bend your knees before falling; the lower you bend them the better it is. Then you roll or hit the wall as you fall." Rolling along the wall helps soften the bumps. Wearing pads also helps soften the bumps.

For Hubie Kerns, even stone or concrete stairs are easy to fall down. "It looks tough," he said. But you put on your elbow, hip, and knee pads and away you go." Yet, sometimes stair falls are made very hard. His son Hubie Kerns, Jr., once went down 100 concrete stairs in a heavy paper box. Hubie, Sr., said that the stunt would have made him gulp twice, even with pads on.

Sometimes the stunt doubles cannot wear pads or wet suits to protect themselves during falls. Hubie, Sr., was not able to wear pads under the tights that were part of Batman's outfit. It is also hard for women to wear pads under costumes like dresses and nightclothes. As Harry Madsen said, "Without pads a stair fall is going to hurt. It's got to hurt. Falling from stair to stair scrapes you up."

Like fights and falls, foot chases are routine for stunt doubles. The "good guys" always chase the "bad guys" on the screen. Foot chases are as carefully planned as car chases. Yet, dangerous spots are sometimes hard to see. In a scene in "A Stranger Is Watching" Vic Magnotta had to run down the railroad tracks as the police chased him. He reached out and pulled himself onto the train just as it left the station. The fourth time Vic ran down the tracks his foot hit a tie that was rotten. The tie collapsed and Vic ended up with a broken bone in his foot.

Several stunt doubles ran down a street in the

disaster movie *Earthquake* as fake bricks and signs fell down. The stunt doubles knew where to run, and the falling objects just missed them. Stephanie Epper was one of the doubles. A fake brick fell near her as planned. Then a cable broke on a sign that was not supposed to fall. It was above Stephanie! Her brother Gary saw it falling, and he pushed her out of the way. Luckily, neither of them was hurt.

The work days of stunt doubles are often filled with surprises. Even light gags like running are a risk!

FALLING FOR DOLLARS

The killer runs through the apartment. He knocks over a chair. He reaches the window and climbs out of it onto the fire ladder. Starsky and Hutch kick in the door. They run to the window. The killer looks over his shoulder and jumps 30 feet (9.1 m) down into the street. He lands on two garbage cans. Starsky and Hutch follow. They jump down and land on the same garbage cans. The noise wakes up the neighborhood. It's a usual scene from the police show "Starsky and Hutch," and it's all a fake. The men who jump out the window are stunt doubles. The garbage cans are made out of plastic. They are "catchers."

Every time stunt doubles fall or jump from a high place they need something to land on. They need a catcher to break the fall. Sometimes the catchers are hidden. The stunt doubles jump to a catcher from a high building. The stars jump 5 or 6 feet (1.5 or 1.8 m) to the ground. When the two pieces of film are put together, the two jumps look like one.

For jumps less than 20 feet (6.1 m), cardboard boxes are the most usual catchers. The air in the empty boxes acts as a cushion. The boxes are piled up, one on top of another. The number of boxes used depends on the number of feet the stunt double will jump. Sometimes mattresses are placed in between the layers of boxes. A mattress is placed on the top and the boxes are tied together. The boxes and mattresses are then covered with a tarpaulin. It holds them firmly in place. If the boxes are not stacked up the right way, the stunt doubles can hit the ground.

In the movie *Superman* Ellen Bry fell into an unusual catcher. She landed on a fruit wagon and smashed $400 worth of watermelons, melons, grapes, and tomatoes. She wore pads and the cart itself was made of styrofoam.

Stunt doubles usually fall onto air bags when they jump more than 20 feet (6.1 m). Air bags are made from good, thick plastic, and they are really two bags in one. The outer bag has small holes in it to let the air out. The inner bag does not have these holes. The usual size of the air bags is 12 to 15 square feet (1.1 to 1.4 sq m), but they are as large as 50 by 100 feet (15.2 by 30.5 m). They are usually 6 feet (1.8 m) deep, but they can be 25 feet (7.6 m) deep.

On the soap opera "Ryan's Hope" the character Delia killed herself. She jumped off a 65-foot (19.8-m) tower in New York City. In real life it was Victoria Vanderkloot who made the jump for the show. It was her first high fall. She said "the tower didn't look real high" at first. But as she practiced for the jump it seemed "the tower started to grow."

Victoria was a little scared on the night of the fall. It was 4:30 in the morning and it was pitch black. She could not see the air bag from the

top of the tower. She said, "It was like jumping into a black hole." But she made the fall and landed safely.

Stunt doubles all agree it is very hard to jump when they cannot see the air bag. In *The Legend of the Lone Ranger* Bob Yerkes made an 80-foot (24.4-m) jump off a cliff. He could not see his air bag. And he had to jump clear of a ledge that stuck out of the cliff!

Many things make falls hard. In the movie, *The Stunt Man*, Gray Johnson fell only 40 feet (12.2 m). But he had to go through a small roof hanging off the building! He had to fall just right to go through the roof and hit the bag.

Vic Magnotta said problems sometimes come up *as the doubles are falling*. He was "shot" and fell off a building in the movie *King of the Gypsies*. He started his six-story fall. Then the blank

Victoria Vanderkloot plunges 65 feet (19.8 m) head first off a tower for the TV soap opera "Ryan's Hope."

from the gun, a wad of paper, bounced off the building and hit his face. He was stunned for the moment and had to use his instincts to fall the right way.

High falls are very, very hard when they are made from planes or helicopters. The double must time the jump just right to land on the air bag. For the TV special "Super Stunts II," Dar Robinson made a record jump. He jumped 311 feet (94.8 m) from a helicopter. That is the same as jumping from the thirty-second floor of a building! He landed on an air bag 50 by 100 feet (15.2 by 30.5 m) wide and 25 feet (7.6 m) deep. The helicopter was unable to stop over it. The wind from the blades would have blown it away or moved it.

A. J. Bakunas jumped 287 feet (87.5 m) from a helicopter to an air bag for *Hooper,* a movie about a stunt man. Then A. J. wanted to break Dar's record. During the making of the movie *Steel,* A. J. jumped 322 feet (98.1 m) from a building to an air bag. He fell through the air at more than 100 mph (160.9 kph). He landed on his air bag, but it had a crack. He went through both layers of it and hit the ground. He died at the age of 29. Because of A. J.'s death, many stunt doubles now put boxes under their air bags. The boxes act as an added layer of protection.

Kitty O'Neil holds the women's record for high jumps. She made three jumps from a helicopter for the TV show "Guinness Book of World Records." On the first jump she fell 130 feet (39.6 m), or 13 stories. On the second jump she fell 160 feet (48.8 m), and the third jump was 180 feet (54.9 m). But her husband, Tom Justice, said, "She'll never do it again. It's too dangerous."

The height of a jump is not the only thing that can make a stunt dangerous. Orwin Harvey fell only 20 feet (6.1 m) from a helicopter to an air bag as the stunt double for Claude Akins on the TV show "Lobo." But he was badly hurt. The suction from the helicopter blades had pulled the air out of the bag, but it looked full. He hit the bag and went right through it. He broke his hip, arm, and leg.

When all goes right, an air bag is a soft catcher. Hitting it is like hitting a pillow. Some catchers are harder. Water is the hardest catcher for high falls. Sometimes hitting the water is like hitting concrete because the stunt doubles cannot make a real dive. Often the doubles are thrown off a boat or a bridge or a cliff. To make the action look real they fall the way they are thrown.

Because very high falls into water are too dangerous, they are sometimes faked. In the western *Butch Cassidy and the Sundance Kid* the posse chases Butch and Sundance, two bank robbers. They ride through the hills and end up at the edge of a cliff, high above a rocky river. Stunt man Joe Canutt really jumped into a net, hanging 10 feet (3 m) below the cliff. The jump into the water was made close to the surface. On the screen the two jumps looked like one.

A jump was also faked in *Saturday Night Fever*, a movie about a disco king. Hank Hooker jumped off the top level of the Verrazano Bridge in New York. He fell 40 feet (12.2 m) to a catcher that stuck out from the bridge. If Hank had missed the catcher, he would have fallen 270 feet (82.3 m) into the water and died.

High jumps are not the only jumps that are hard. Roof-to-roof jumps are also dangerous. Bob

Minor doubled Sidney Poitier in *Let's Do It Again*, a movie about two con artists. In one scene Bob had to jump from the roof of one building to the roof of a building 18½ feet (5.6 m) away and 2 feet (.6 m) lower. He was 130 feet (39.6 m) above the ground and had no catcher between the buildings. He made the jump at 2 A.M. Over 200 people came to see him jump. He ran up a 34-inch (86.4-cm) ramp, raised his head up high, stretched his body out, and pushed off. He said, "I sailed through the air like a bird. In fact, my friends call me Minor bird." He jumped 24½ feet (7.4 m) and the crowd cheered. He said, "It was wonderful. It was a thrill I will never forget."

Dar Robinson will never forget his most dangerous jump, either. He jumped off the Canadian National (CN) Tower in Toronto, Canada, for the movie *High Point*. The CN Tower is the world's tallest structure; it is 1,178 feet (359 m) high. Dar jumped off it and fell free for six seconds. Then he pulled the string on his parachute. It took three seconds to open fully. In one more second he would have hit the ground.

High falls are dangerous. They are done only

by stunt doubles who have perfect timing. The doubles need to land the right way or they can break their backs, their legs, or their arms. Even when the catcher is an air bag, it is important to fall the right way and it takes practice. Hal Needham said the secret to falling is to be "looser than warm spaghetti."

LOOK, UP IN THE SKY! IT'S A STUNT DOUBLE!

"A heart stopper" is what Gary Epper called an air stunt for the TV show "240-Robert." The show was based on the real-life work of the Los Angeles Sheriff's Search and Rescue Unit. For one episode Gary hung from a wire between two trees. He was 100 feet (30.5 m) above the ground. A helicopter pilot flew in to "rescue" him. He dropped Gary a line. Gary tied the line around himself and cut the wire from which he had hung. The helicopter started to airlift him up. Suddenly, the stunt went wrong.

The helicopter was caught by a wind and changed direction. Gary ended up in the top of the trees instead of over them. The line got caught in the branches, and Gary was not able to swing free. By radio he told the pilot to hold the chopper in one place. Gary worked the lines loose and the gag was redone. He was not hurt, but he could have been snapped in two if the chopper had flown off while he was tangled in the trees.

Helicopter rescue scenes are common in movies and on television. Because helicopters are able to remain in the air in one spot, they are used in real life and "reel life" to pick people up. They rescue people from ships, buildings, mountains, and more.

Water pickups are the hardest for stunt doubles to do. Usually, the stunt doubles wear scuba or deep-sea diving gear. They are unable to move freely in the diving suits, and they cannot reach very high out of the water. The helicopter pilot has to come down close to the water—but not too close. If a skid or runner of the chopper dips under the water, it can pull the whole helicopter down.

Sometimes helicopters pick up things besides

people. Of course, people are sometimes inside these things! On "Wonder Woman" a helicopter picked up a telephone booth. Inside the booth was Jeannie Epper, the stunt double for the star, Lynda Carter. The pilot lifted the telephone booth 4 feet (1.2 m) above the ground. Then he set it down and Jeannie climbed out. A dummy was put inside the booth, and the pilot flew off again. On the show it looked as though he flew far away with Wonder Woman in the telephone booth.

On the TV show "The Fall Guys" a helicopter supposedly picked up a car full of "bad guys." The helicopter lifted it up with a huge hook. But the car in the air was not real. It was a fake car made out of plastic.

Stunt doubles often climb down from helicopters to cars or trains. They transfer from the chopper to cars, trucks, or trains going as fast as 40 or 50 mph (64.4 or 80.5 kmph). David Ellis said, "Good helicopter pilots can fly above the top of the car. They can set you down on the car as though it is standing still."

Helicopters are harder to fly than airplanes. Helicopters can be blown off course by the wind.

They often have more mechanical problems than planes. They sometimes overheat. Then the engines stop. Tony Epper said it gives stunt doubles a scare when they are hanging under an overheated helicopter. But the stunt doubles and the pilots plan for problems. They choose a place where the helicopter can set the stunt doubles down if something goes wrong.

Ross Reynolds, a pilot, said something does go wrong once in a while. But good pilots learn to handle problems and hard stunts. Ross has done a number of exciting and dangerous air stunts. On "The Rockford Files" he chased a car in his helicopter. They went 60 mph (96.6 kmph) through an airplane hangar at an airfield. He flew low because he needed space above the blades. He said there was "nothing" to the stunt; it was easy. But it took careful planning and perfect weather. When a wind blows across the hangar door, the stunt is too dangerous to do. Outside the hangar the pilot fixes the controls to fly in the wind. Inside the hangar there is no wind. The helicopter can go into a spin and crash.

Flying an old plane through a hangar is also

dangerous. Paul Mantz flew a fake World War I airplane through a hangar for the movie *It's a Mad, Mad, Mad, Mad World*. The wind blew across the doors at each end of the hangar! It was a hard flight. But Paul Mantz was one of the best pilots in movie history.

It's a Mad, Mad, Mad, Mad World is a funny movie about several people searching for money hidden by bank robbers. In this movie, Paul Mantz and his partner, Frank Tallman, performed several air stunts. Frank Tallman did one that was very dangerous. He flew a fake World War I biplane through a large sign, or billboard. The frame of the billboard was made out of steel. The billboard itself was made of light paper for the movie. But it was too light. It moved in the wind. The billboard was built again out of balsa wood and 3-inch (7.6-cm) styrofoam. It still moved in the wind. Three more inches of styrofoam were added. Finally, it stopped moving and Frank Tallman flew through it. The wings of the plane broke, the propellers moved off center, and the front window cracked. Styrofoam and balsa wood wrapped around parts of the plane. The plane also overheated. Another pilot might have crashed. But Tallman landed safe and sound.

Most helicopter and airplane crashes are faked for the screen. Someone yells, "Look the plane is crashing." Then the next scene shows a plane on the ground all smashed up. Airplane crashes are dangerous and expensive. Helicopter crashes are very dangerous because the spinning blades fly off in all directions.

In *The Great Waldo Pepper* three airplane crashes were really done for the movie. The same 1917 plane was used for all three of them! Robert Redford starred as Waldo Pepper, a stunt pilot, or "barnstormer," of the 1920s. Waldo traveled from air show to air show to do stunts. He imagined fighting the Red Baron, the top German pilot during World War I. The movie, of course, has several good air stunts in it. Pilot Jim Appleby flew for Redford.

For the three crashes an old biplane was used. It was rebuilt from old spare parts. Like crash cars, the plane was padded. Extra metal or armor plate lined the plane to make it stronger. The gasoline tank was moved away from the cockpit to lessen the danger of a fire near the pilot.

Then the wings were cut a little to make them fall off when the plane crashed.

Some low-altitude air stunts in *The Great Waldo Pepper* were even more dangerous than the crashes. Frank Tallman made several flights close to the ground. In one scene he was asked to fly down the street as close to the ground as possible. He flew the plane 6 inches (15.2 cm) above the ground! But on film it looked as though the plane was on the ground, not above it. To improve that, he made the flight again 6 feet (1.8 m) above the ground. This time the color of the sky was wrong for the scene. He was asked to make the flight again. In all, he flew the dangerous stunt eight times.

Pilot Art Scholl also flew in *The Great Waldo Pepper*. He explained the danger of low flights: "If you make a mistake, you hit the ground. If you're up high, you have time to correct a mistake." When he flew a stunt called an "outside loop" in the plane, he was only 10 feet (3 m) off the ground. For the stunt he flew the plane in a circle, nose over tail. The plane was upside down at one point during the stunt.

In 1980 Art Scholl flew his most dangerous

stunt on "That's Incredible." He flew a DeHavilland plane in a loop and went under a ribbon upside down. The tail of the plane was only 5 feet (1.5 m) off the ground. The force of gravity was great. It nearly pulled him out of the plane.

Art Scholl as the Red Baron and Jim Appleby as Redford's double in *The Great Waldo Pepper* fought an air battle. It, too, was a dangerous stunt. During the battle Appleby flew into a ravine. It was 150 feet (45.7 m) wide and about 2,500 feet (762 m) long. Then Scholl flew into it and disappeared. Soon they both reappeared. Jim Appleby said, "In the ravine we were 50 feet [15.2 m] below the ground. There was no wind. When the planes went back up, they were hit with wind. With only 15 to 20 feet [4.6 to 6.1 m] of space on either side of them, the planes had to be flown exactly right. That's what made the stunt

Frank Tallman flew a World War I biplane down a street for the movie The Great Waldo Pepper.

very dangerous." Flying through the ravine was like flying through a hangar.

Sometimes the flights are dangerous for the pilots. But more often air stunts are dangerous for the stunt doubles. They are the ones who hang below the plane or helicopter or who jump or climb out of them. To protect the stunt doubles, the pilots carefully plan the gags with them.

HIT ME

"It's a strange feeling to hear the roar of the flames and to know it's you that is burning," said Harry Madsen. As Michael Quinn's double, he was turned into a human torch for the horror movie *Echoes*. He played a man who set himself on fire and then set the room on fire with his own body.

Fire stunts are very dangerous. Stunt doubles are protected from the flames, but the heat builds up quickly. Victoria Vanderkloot said, "You almost cook." Throughout fire gags, safety persons are on the set. They hold the fire extinguishers or blankets to smother the flames. They put out the flames the second the scene ends. Once in a while the stunt doubles burn too fast or too much to finish the scene. They then signal or scream, "Hit me," which means put out the fire.

Stunt doubles use either a special fire-resistant gel or fire-resistant clothes to protect their skin from the flames. When the gel is used, the burns look more real than when the clothes are worn. The clothes sometimes look too thick. The special gel acts as a shield, and it keeps the double's skin from burning. It also lowers the temperature of the double's body.

In the science fiction movie *Scanners*, Celine Fournier did an exciting fire stunt. She covered herself with the special gel from head to toe. Then she put on her costume, a short dress. Some parts of the dress were smeared with a substance that burns fast. The cameras started rolling (working). Then the substance was set on fire, and the entire dress burned up. As soon as the scene ended, she

Harry Madsen was set on fire in the horror film Echoes.

was covered with foam from the extinguisher. It took only seconds for the fire to go out.

Vic Magnotta used the gel for fire stunts in *Wolfen* and *Fort Apache, The Bronx*. They were extremely dangerous stunts. He set his face on fire! First, he smeared the gel all over his face and hair. Then he put small dabs of a flammable or fast-burning, substance over the gel on his face. After the cameras started to roll, the flammable substance was set on fire. Sometimes the substance that burns drips. Vic had to be very, very careful not to let it drip into his eyes.

Many stunt doubles like to use fire-resistant clothes instead of the gel. As Victoria Vanderkloot said, "There's nothing between your flesh and the flames except the gel." It is possible for the gel to dry out during a gag. It does not work well when it is dry. The gel also costs a lot.

The fire-resistant clothes are made from Nomex. It is a light, soft material used for racing car suits. The white Nomex clothes look like long underwear. The openings of the clothes are carefully taped shut. The taped openings keep the flames from licking up or coming up inside the clothes and burning the stunt double's skin.

Several suits of fire-resistant clothes are worn for burns of more than 20 or 30 seconds. Kitty O'Neil wore six layers of clothes for a combination high fall and burn on a TV special. The top suit of clothes was coated with a fireproof chemical. Then the back of the suit was coated with a flammable substance. Kitty was set on fire and jumped 90 feet (27.4 m) to an air bag. The flames were put out when she hit the bag. Kitty's burn was known as a partial burn. Only one part of her—her back—was burned.

Most of the burns on the screen are partial burns. Usually the flames are behind the stunt doubles, where they cannot flare up in their faces. Sometimes, an overhead fan is used to blow the flames away from the double's face.

Sometimes stunt doubles have to run out of burning houses. They may be in flames from head to toe. For these full burns they wear special fire-resistant suits including hoods that cover their heads and faces. The longer a fire burns, the hotter it gets. The sweat which pours off the stunt doubles can turn into steam and can give them second-degree burns. During full burns the temperature of the air around them reaches 200° to 900° F (93°

to 482° C). Hal Needham said, "If they breathe the air around them, it will be all over. Their lungs will burn."

But the doubles have to breathe! Inside their hoods are bottles of compressed air. Usually the bottles have three minutes of air in them. Sometimes they have six minutes of air. But the more air, the larger the bottle. The larger bottles make it hard for the doubles to move.

The doubles usually "burn" for only 10 to 30 seconds. A 45-second burn is a "big burn," for the heat builds up fast. But stunt doubles need more than 30 to 45 seconds of air to breathe. The rest of the air is needed while they prepare for the burn and while the fire is being put out. One stunt man said he once ran out of air. His cheeks puffed up and his eyes bulged out.

The Towering Inferno is a disaster movie about a fire in a tall building, or skyscraper. It contains many dangerous fire stunts. The most dangerous fire gag was done by Mike Johnson. He ran through several burning rooms without an air bottle. Paul Stader planned the stunt. He said, "The fire was so hot Mike had to run holding his breath. If he'd have fallen, it would have been very hard to save his life." Fire stunts are planned with care and practiced. In the thick smoke the doubles cannot see where they are going. They must move the way they practiced.

The excitement of *The Towering Inferno* was created by great stunts and special effects. Burning a high-rise building was not possible. Instead a 70-foot (21.3-m) miniature building was burned. Tanks pumped butane or liquid gas to jets hidden in the back of the building. The jets worked like the jets on a gas stove. They were turned on and off as needed. As soon as they were turned off, the fire died. The burning liquid gas was pumped through pipes lining the windows and doors. When the flames leaped out the windows, it made it look as though the whole building was burning. In most movies and TV shows, fires are created the same way.

In *Urban Cowboy* Gene Hartline fell 35 feet (10.7 m) to a catwalk and caught on fire. He was doubling Barry Corbin. He walked up the stairs to check an oil tank. Lightning struck. Two oil tanks burst into flames. Then Gene fell. He was surrounded by gas pipes. The flames shot out of the gas pipes and set his costume on fire. His costume had been painted with a flammable substance.

The oil tanks were burned like the buildings in *The Towering Inferno*. Liquid gas was pumped into the tanks and set on fire. Gene said that the heat from both the tanks and the pipes was very, very hot. At the end of the gag the fire on his body was put out. The jets to the tanks and pipes were turned off. But he said, "The stunt took 20 to 30 seconds. Yet I cooked like a lobster. I was red for three days."

Hank Hooker also did a fire stunt in which the heat was very, very high. He burned for more than a minute on "Games People Play." He sat in a car wearing a fire suit with a hood. His air tank had six minutes of air. The car burst into flames when six gasoline bombs in it were set off. Gunpowder charges blew off the doors, the truck lid, and the hood. Hank's suit had been covered with a flammable substance. The flames from the burning car set him on fire. He then ran out of the car. It was the first time this gag had been done. But he said, "I was not worried. My brother Joe was my safety man."

As a joke Gene Hartline said, "Don't use safety guards who owe you money." But he knows safety is no laughing matter. The lives of the stunt doubles are in the hands of the safety persons. The heat builds up fast. Within seconds, stunt doubles can be burned. All fire stunts are dangerous.

GLUB! GLUB!

"As the water came at us, it sounded like the roar of the ocean," said Jeannie Epper. She was one of 18 stunt doubles in a water scene in the disaster movie *Earthquake*. They played people who were washed down a large storm drain in Los Angeles. The walls of the fake drain were 10 feet (3 m) high. They went straight up. There was no way out for the stunt doubles. The doubles stood in this drain and waited for thousands of gallons of water to come pouring through.

Jeannie saw 17 sets of eyes. They were wide open and filled with fear. She said, "I looked at them and I looked at the wall of water as it came at us. I thought, 'We're in trouble.' The water hit us so hard it knocked us down. Our knees got scraped. It was really frightening."

Then the stunt doubles were asked to do the scene again. They were all scared. Jeannie decided, "I'm going to do it and ride it out." But she now feels that "it took a lot more guts than brains" to do the scene again.

Water stunts are sometimes very dangerous. The force of large amounts of rushing water is great. In *The Towering Inferno* a nightclub is flooded with water from the water tank on top of the building. The stunt doubles were hit with 8,000 gallons (30,320 l) of water. They hung onto the props. They never felt the full force of the water. As the water was poured out of the tanks, it hit a barrier. Then it hit the doubles.

Paul Stader said stunt doubles never feel the full force of the water in flood scenes. Yet stunt doubles are sometimes knocked down by the water. Sometimes they are knocked into the sets. Sometimes the props are washed into them. The problem for the stunt doubles is not knowing what

will happen. They cannot plan the stunts in water as well as other gags. As Bob Yerkes said, "You hope for the best." He was among the doubles swept down the aisle of a plane in the movie *Airport '79.*

Kitty O'Neil was also swept down the aisle in *Airport '79.* She said she swallowed some of the water as it poured into the "cabin" of the plane. The water was very cold and the scene took almost an hour to finish. Kitty was sick afterward. Water stunts are not only dangerous, they are often unpleasant, too, especially on cold days.

The water stunts in *The Poseidon Adventure* are among the best ever seen in a movie. It is a story about a ship that is turned over by a 90-foot (27.4-m) tidal wave. When the tidal wave hit, the ballroom of the ship was flooded. Over 100 stunt doubles were in the scene. They were hit with

In a scene from the movie Earthquake, *eighteen stunt doubles were washed down a storm drain.*

water shot out of six compressed-air cannons. The set was built to hold up to 4 feet (1.2 m) of water. It looked as though the force of the water broke the windows in the ballroom. They were really broken by tiny charges or explosives around them. The windows were made out of candy glass.

In the next scene the ballroom slowly turned, as the ship turned over on its side. The set was built to move. The tables were nailed down. Nine stunt doubles held on to the tables. Then one by one, they dropped into the water. The stunt planner, Paul Stader, said it was very dangerous because each of the nine people had to fall at just the right time. But the stunt doubles all fell at the right moments, and no one was hurt.

Paul himself did a dangerous stunt. He played the ship's telegraph operator in *The Poseidon Adventure*. As he was calling for help, the cabin was flooded. The set was carefully planned for the stunt. Paul said that the cabin was on a set that moved around in a circle. On the top of the set was a tank of water. The set turned as the water was let out of the tank. The turning kept the water from hitting Paul too hard. But he said, "It was still very dangerous." The force of the water could have knocked him down—or could even have knocked the breath out of him.

Hubie Kerns, Sr., lost his breath when he was in *The Ten Commandments.* When the Red Sea closed, he was the only soldier standing on the banks. The force of the water as the two sides of the river came together was great. He said, "The water just shot me up to the top like a cork." The director wanted Hubie to get washed down the river by the water. He had hoses put under the water to shoot the stunt man from one side of the tank to the other. As Hubie was shot from side to side, he lost his breath. But he dived to the bottom of the tank and kicked himself up. He said, "I almost opened my mouth for air before I got to the top. I was far gone."

Hank Wills worked out a way to breathe underwater for the movie *Houdini.* This movie was about a man named Harry Houdini, who was a master of escape. In real life, he could get out of trunks that were locked and lowered into water. He could get out of tanks while he was in chains. Houdini could escape from all kinds of things in all kinds of places. As the double for Tony Curtis, Hank re-created Houdini's escapes.

One stunt was an escape from a river covered with ice. The scene was really filmed in a large 150-feet (45.7-m) tank at the studio. Fake ice was made from wax. To make it look like real ice, the wax ice had holes in it. The holes were 6 to 8 inches (15.2 to 20.3 cm) above the water. Hank was able to breathe the air in these holes as he did the scene!

Many water stunts are done in large tanks at the studio. But some water stunts are done in real lakes, rivers, or oceans. Often, the stunt doubles find they have problems when they work outside the studio, on location.

Dar Robinson worked on location in a swamp in Georgia. He doubled Steve McQueen in the movie *Papillon*, which was about escaped prisoners. Dar fought a crocodile in the swampy water —a live crocodile! The legs of the crocodile were tied and its mouth was wired shut. But he was still dangerous. Dar said, "The crocodile turned every which way but loose. I was on top of him, under him, and all over him. I drank half of the yellow, green, brown pond. It was bad! It made me sick."

Gary Epper worked on location in Hawaii for the police show "Hawaii Five-O." He once crashed a car into water. When it sank to the bottom, Gary looked out the car window. He saw hammerhead sharks 25 feet (7.6 m) away. He said that he did not want to get out of the car. But he finally climbed out the window and moved slowly up. The sharks moved, too—away from him.

In *Jaws* Ted Grossman was bitten by a shark, a mechanical shark named Orca. It had two kinds of teeth. Its rubber teeth were for biting people. Its plastic teeth were for biting boats, barrels, and other things. When Orca lost a number of rubber teeth, they were replaced by plastic teeth. No one told Ted. He fought the shark for a long time in one scene. He then came out of the water. Blood was slowly dripping down his leg. He yelled out, "Look, it really bit me!"

AS EASY AS FALLING OFF A HORSE

He pulls up his boots. He gives the dance hall girl a kiss. He runs out to the balcony and jumps 10 feet (3 m) down to his horse, ready to ride out of town. The scene is almost the same in western after western, from the classic movies like *Stagecoach* to TV shows like "Gunsmoke" or "Bret Maverick."

Of course, it is the stunt person who really jumps onto the horse. Andy Epper said that it's really easy if it is done the right way. Andy should know. He started doing western gags as a child on the TV show "My Friend Flicka." He said, "The secret to jumping onto a horse is to keep your knees in. You 'catch' the horse near his front legs with the inside of your knees. Then you sit down." He also added, "Not everyone knows how to do it." If the jump is done wrong, both the horse and the stunt double can get hurt.

Once on the horse, the western "good guy," or hero, sometimes chases the "bad guy." Chases look like easy gags. They are—unless the horse falls down. During a chase for *The Legend of the Lone Ranger*, Andy Epper's horse stepped into a gopher hole that was covered with grass. It was the first time his horse had ever fallen. He said, "Down we went. I hurt my ribs, my shoulder, and my back."

Usually, it is Andy who falls down when he is "shot." Sometimes falling off a horse is as easy as falling off a log—but not always. He said that horse falls can be dangerous. After the stunt dou-

Over: John Epper, Andy's father, jumped his horse, Bracket, in a 1948 western.

bles fall, the horse can kick them or step on them by mistake.

For falls from horses, stunt doubles use L-shaped stirrups to push themselves out of the saddle. They plan the exact spot, or "mark," where they will fall off. They soften the ground around the mark with sand. They also wear pads on the tailbone, elbows, and knees.

Once, Hank Wills was hurt when he did not wear pads. He was working on the movie *The Fighting Kentuckians*. He was asked to fall off a horse, a stunt that had not been planned. He did not have his pads with him. But he had often done falls without pads and never been hurt. This time he fell off the horse and broke his hip. He was out of work for 11 months.

On the set of *One Eyed Jacks* Hank was hurt a second time. His horse fell on top of him, and the saddle horn hit him in the stomach. He was out of work for four months. Yet Hank calls himself lucky! He has done over 1,400 horse gags in over 40 years of working as a stunt man. He has been hurt only twice.

In the movie *Stagecoach* Yakima Canutt

made a fall that had never been tried. He played an Indian and he jumped from a running horse onto the lead horse pulling the stagecoach. As he pulled the reins, he was "shot" by the driver. He fell to the ground between two speeding horses. Hanging on to the tongue of the stagecoach, he was dragged on the ground on his back. He was "shot" again. He let go of the tongue as the six horses and the coach passed over him. The horses were running at 45 mph (72.4 kmph) and they were only 3 feet (.9 m) from one another. He said it was "a gag you could easily rub yourself out with if you make the wrong move." He did not.

Yakima's famous stunt was imitated in the popular movie *Raiders of the Lost Ark*. But Terry Leonard fell under a truck, which passed over him. He then climbed back up. The stunt was as dangerous as the western gag.

The riders do not always fall off their horses. Sometimes they are pulled off by a wire or cable. The thin wire cannot be seen on the screen. Stunt doubles are often "shot" off their horses.

Gunshots are made from real powder charges called squibs. The tiny charges are hidden behind walls, benches, or other things. They are set off by remote control when the shot is fired. When they go off, it looks as if a bullet hit.

For gunshot wounds, a squib is taped to a metal plate. The plate is sewn into the clothing. Then rubber sacs of fake blood are taped over the squib. When the squib goes off, the sac breaks and the "blood" pours out. Fake blood is often made from corn syrup and red food color. The thick syrup works well because it drips slowly. Because the "blood" is sometimes put into stunt doubles' mouths, it must be safe to eat.

Sometimes it is not the rider but the horse that falls down. Today most horses are trained to fall down, but once in a while they are tripped. They are tripped by a cable called a Running W. It is a cable with three small rings that go around the horse's feet. When the horse gallops off, the

In the movie Stagecoach, *a Running W was used to make the horse fall.*

cable is pulled tight. When the end of the cable is reached, the horse trips and falls down. The sudden fall is hard on both the rider and the horse.

The Running W was often used during the 1930s. During those years John Epper doubled most of the best western stars, including Ronald Reagan and Gary Cooper. He said, "I've seen horses get killed when they were tripped by Running W's. Even in the 30s we had no need for Running W's. We had horses trained to fall. The horses fell into a deep bed of moss and they did not get hurt."

For years the American Humane Association (AHA) asked the movie studios not to use Running W's. Finally, the studios agreed in 1939. But once in a while the Running W is still used. Once in a while a horse is hurt or even killed.

Most people who plan stunts with horses take care not to hurt the animals. Super horse stunts that look dangerous are usually safe. In the film *Major Dundee* 23 western soldiers on horses looked as though they were blown up by cannons. But they were not! Hank Wills planned the stunt. He said that a dam was built next to the banks of the river. The horses ran through water 1 foot (.3 m) high. Then they reached a spot where it suddenly was 4 feet (1.2 m) high. It looked as though the horses had been hit and had fallen. Yet during the stunt, he said, "Not one horse really fell."

Working with horses in water is hard. John Epper said, "If a horse gets water into his lungs, he's gone." His hardest stunt was jumping a horse 20 feet (6.1 m) off a bridge into a lake for the Elvis Presley movie *Love Me Tender.* A horse sometimes falls over on its side when it lands in water. If it falls over, it can trap the rider under the water or get water into its own lungs.

A horse almost drowned when the movie *High Point* was made. Hank Wills drove a horse and wagon off a 20-foot (6.1-m) high pier into the St. Lawrence River in Canada. The riverbanks went straight up. Wills needed a way to get the horse out of the river. He had a ramp built. He put it on a flat boat in the river and lowered it into the water. He placed a fake horse on the ramp to make the real horse swim to it. The boat was about 150 feet (45.7 m) away from where they went off the pier. Four life belts were around the horse's body. They were painted the same color as the horse's coat. As the wagon sailed through the air, a cable was opened to free the horse.

But Wills said that the unexpected happened. After they hit the water, he waited a long, long time for the horse to come up. When the horse came to the top of the water, it swam away from the boat instead of toward it. Wills grabbed one of the long reins and tugged on it. He pointed the horse in the right direction.

Yet, Wills knew something was still wrong. The horse had practiced the swim many times. But it had trouble keeping its nose above the water. The horse looked scared. Then it sank under the water. Wills pulled at the reins and it came up. Wills said, "I yelled and I prayed. And I kept giving him short tugs. Then he saw the fake horse on the ramp. He used all his strength to reach it." Then Wills learned the cable had circled around the horse's back leg. The horse had pulled the wagon under the water the whole way!

Once in a while a stunt will not work as it was planned. But the best stunt doubles never plan a stunt that is dangerous for the horse or for them. They love their horses and protect them.

SO YOU WANT TO BE A STUNT DOUBLE

The angels on "Charlie's Angels" went undercover as stunt women on a movie set in Hollywood. BJ on "BJ and the Bear" went undercover as a stunt man. For them it was easy to become stunt doubles. But in real life it is not easy. It is very hard. It takes athletic skills, brains, and "guts" to become a stunt double.

Many stunt men and women are former athletes, like Kitty O'Neil. Some of them are former circus performers, like Dar Robinson, Sandy Alexander, and Bob Yerkes. Some, like Harry Madsen, once worked as rodeo performers. They often have had "physical" jobs because stunt doubles need coordination.

Harry Madsen said stunt doubles also need to think well, to take directions, and to work well with others. It is important for stunt doubles to think fast when a stunt goes wrong.

Stunt schools are popping up all over the country. Some of them are only rip-offs. The best schools are run by working stunt doubles. They teach students such stunts as falling, fighting, riding, and climbing. But jobs are still very hard to find.

Stunt doubles like to work with men and women they know are good. Their lives are sometimes in the hands of their co-workers. Most often stunt doubles work with members of their own groups. The best-known groups in Hollywood are the Stuntmen's Association of Motion Pictures and Stunts Unlimited. In New York the best-known group is the East Coast Stuntmen's Association. Very few stunt doubles are asked to join the groups.

Stunt work is often handed down from parents to their children. Parents are able to teach their children how to do stunts. They are also able to help them get jobs. John Epper's six children— Tony, Andy, Gary, Stephanie, Margo, and Jeannie —all became stunt doubles. Only Margo no longer does stunts. Now Jeannie's children Richard and Kurtis are working as stunt doubles. Kurtis is only 13! Stephanie's daughter Kim also works as a stunt double.

Hugh Hooker's sons Hank and Buddy Joe worked as stunt doubles before they were ten years old. Hank did his first heavy, or hard, stunt at the age of nine. On the TV show "Rin Tin Tin" he roped a wild horse. Hank said, "It dragged me 150 feet [45.7 m] across hard ground and rocks. My chest was covered with a steel plate, called a sled. I was supposed to let go of the rope about 3 feet [.9 m] from a large rock. But I was scared. I never let go of the rope until I was only inches away from the rock. The drag tore the whole sled apart. My face was covered with dirt except for two tear lines. I was really scared, but I loved it, too."

Once in a while stunt doubles teach an apprentice, or beginner. They teach them all the

tricks of the trade. But the apprentices need to train and to practice very hard.

Stunt doubles are paid $298 per day or $1,038 per week. They are also paid a fee for each gag. The fees are called adjustments, and they are paid every time the stunt is done. The more dangerous the stunt is, the more money the stunt double earns. Jerry Summers once did the same gag 23 times. He walked the wing of an old airplance and earned over $19,000.

The top stunt men earn $100,000 per year or more. But stunt doubles who are new in the business often earn very, very little. Some stunt doubles also coordinate or plan all the stunts for a movie or TV show. They earn between $100,000

Kurtis Sanders, age 13, is the son of Jeannie Epper and the grandson of retired stunt man John Epper. He is the third generation of the Epper family to work as a stunt double. He jumped from a height of 30 feet (9.1 m) onto an air bag.

and $200,000 per year. But they work hard. Hank Wills planned almost 350 stunts for the movie *Major Dundee*!

Many stunt coordinators or planners later work as second-unit directors. They direct all the action scenes. They often earn between $150,000 and $250,000.

Very few women earn over $50,000, and even fewer (about five or six) earn $50,00 to $100,000. Because the "bad guys," police, and ranchers are usually men, there is less work for stunt women. Even the stunts supposedly done by women characters are often done by men dressed as women. Hank Hooker said, "Most directors will not give a woman a 'heavy,' 'heavy' stunt to do." The more dangerous the stunt, the more it pays.

Jeannie Epper feels that women have come a long way. But "the stunt world is still a man's world. They won't give us the ball and let us run with it."

More and more young men and women want to become stunt doubles. More and more of them also want to make names for themselves. Some of them are taking too many chances. A. J. Bakunas said, "I've never turned down a job. When other stunt men don't want to do a job, they call me." He took chances and it cost him his life.

A few directors push the stunt doubles to do dangerous stunts. Hank Wills said, "Some of them think stunt men are supermen." But most stunt doubles do not take chances. They want the stunts to look exciting. They also want the stunts to be done safely.

Still stunt doubles often get bruises or broken bones. Pain is part of the job. Some stunt doubles have broken many bones many times. Some agree with Harry Madsen. He said, "I've broken ribs, but gee, that hardly counts." And still others have never broken a bone.

Stunt doubles are usually more careful as they get older. It takes longer for them to heal. Duffy Hambleton is in his mid-forties. He said, "I used to pack my bag, jump on a plane, and go out to locations without asking about the stunts." Now he asks!

Going out to locations or to the places where the films are made is a good part of the work and a bad part. Sometimes the stunt doubles work in exciting cities. Sometimes they work in a desert or a jungle.

But working in different places on different stunts makes the job exciting. The danger also makes the job exciting. As Hubie Kerns said, "Stunt work is fun. It's like not working."

GLOSSARY

Camera angle—The angle at which the camera is pointed at whatever is being filmed.

Closeup—A shot of the person's face only.

Cut—A change from one camera angle to another. Also the term used by the director to stop the action.

Director—The person in charge of all the work on a film.

Double—A person who takes the place of the actor or actress for a particular scene.

Dub—To put dialogue or sounds on film after it has been shot.

Edit—To put shots together into a movie or program.

Location—A place away from the studio where the film is shot.

Long shot—A shot seen from a distance.

Prop—Any object on the set, from a goldfish to a table. Breakaway props are made out of materials that break easily.

Script—The written play for the movie or TV program.

Second unit director—The person in charge of the action scenes.

Scene—A series of shots or a single shot that takes place in a single location and deals with a single action.

Shot—A short series or sequence of pictures, taken with a single movie or TV camera.

Special effects—A wide range of props such as rain, models of buildings, explosions, fires, and pieces of equipment that are created especially for the movies or TV, and look like the real thing on film.

Stunt—An action such as falling down a flight of stairs.

Take—A shot. The word is also used to number the times a shot has been made, such as "Take Four."